W9-CRZ-492

VANCOUVER PUBLIC LIBRARY

Big
Science Ideas

How do animals communicate?

Bobbie Kalman

🌳 Crabtree Publishing Company

www.crabtreebooks.com

Big Science Ideas

Created by Bobbie Kalman

For John and Jill Wiens,
whose Riverbend Inn is our second home
and "guest house"

**Author and
Editor-in-Chief**
Bobbie Kalman

Editor
Kathy Middleton

Proofreader
Crystal Sikkens

Design
Bobbie Kalman
Katherine Berti
Samantha Crabtree (cover)

Production coordinator
Katherine Berti

Illustrations
Barbara Bedell: page 24

Photographs and reproductions
© BigStockPhoto.com: page 25 (inset)
© Dreamstime.com: pages 17 (bottom right),
    21 (bottom left), 25 (top)
© iStockphoto.com: page 27 (top)
© Shutterstock.com: cover, pages 1, 3, 4, 5, 6, 7, 8, 9, 11, 12, 13, 14,
    15, 16, 17 (except bottom right), 18, 19, 20, 21 (except bottom left),
    22, 23, 24, 25 (bottom), 26, 27 (bottom), 28, 29, 30, 31
© Robert Thomas: page 10

Library and Archives Canada Cataloguing in Publication

Kalman, Bobbie, 1947-
    How do animals communicate? / Bobbie Kalman.

(Big science ideas)
Includes index.
ISBN 978-0-7787-3282-2 (bound).--ISBN 978-0-7787-3302-7 (pbk.)

    1. Animal communication--Juvenile literature. I. Title. II. Series:
Kalman, Bobbie, 1947- . Big science ideas.

QL776.K343 2009   j591.59   C2009-901255-3

Library of Congress Cataloging-in-Publication Data

Kalman, Bobbie.
    How do animals communicate? / Bobbie Kalman.
        p. cm. -- (Big science ideas)
    Includes index.
    ISBN 978-0-7787-3302-7 (pbk. : alk. paper) -- ISBN 978-0-7787-3282-2
(reinforced library binding : alk. paper)
    1. Animal communication--Juvenile literature. I. Title. II. Series.

    QL776.K343 2009
    591.59--dc22
                                                    2009008002

Crabtree Publishing Company

www.crabtreebooks.com   1-800-387-7650
Copyright © **2009 CRABTREE PUBLISHING COMPANY**. All rights reserved. No part of this publication may be reproduced, stored in a
retrieval system or be transmitted in any form or by any means, electronic, mechanical, photocopying, recording, or otherwise, without the prior
written permission of Crabtree Publishing Company. In Canada: We acknowledge the financial support of the Government of Canada through the
Book Publishing Industry Development Program (BPIDP) for our publishing activities.

Published in Canada
Crabtree Publishing
616 Welland Ave.
St. Catharines, Ontario
L2M 5V6

Published in the United States
Crabtree Publishing
PMB16A
350 Fifth Ave., Suite 3308
New York, NY 10118

Published in the United Kingdom
Crabtree Publishing
White Cross Mills
High Town, Lancaster
LA1 4XS

Published in Australia
Crabtree Publishing
386 Mt. Alexander Rd.
Ascot Vale (Melbourne)
VIC 3032

Contents

What is communication?

To **communicate** is to exchange information, ideas, dreams, and feelings with others. People communicate to teach, to ask others to do something, to show feelings, to warn others of danger, and to entertain. People communicate by talking, writing, drawing or taking pictures, making movies, and creating music.

This teacher is teaching a student. She is sharing her knowledge and ideas. The student is writing down the information she has learned. She will read it to the class. In which three ways are the teacher and student communicating?

Using body language

People also use **body language** to communicate how they feel. They laugh, frown, and **gesture** with their hands and heads. What are these children communicating through their body language?

5

Do animals communicate?

*The bright colors of poison dart frogs warn **predators** that eating these frogs will kill them.*

Just like people, animals also need to share information. They communicate where to find food and warn one another of danger. They also use communication to attract **mates**.

Do animals talk?

Animals cannot use words or read, but they can communicate! They use senses such as sight, smell, taste, hearing, and touch to send and receive messages. Some animals make sounds that scare others. Other animals use colors and **patterns** to attract other animals or scare them away.

Hippopotamuses growl, grunt, and bellow to scare away enemies. They often attack crocodiles, which live in the same rivers as the hippos.

Animal body language

Animals also use body language to communicate with one another. They use different body parts to send messages. Some messages are friendly, and some show fear or anger. Some are warning signals.

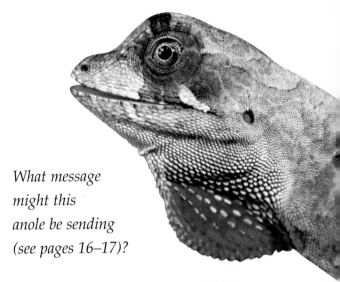

What message might this anole be sending (see pages 16–17)?

*What message are these **calves**, or baby cows, giving each other?*

Roars, growls, and howls

Many animals make very loud sounds that scare other animals away. Tigers and lions are big cats that have long **larynxes**, or voiceboxes. Long larynxes allow these cats to make loud, long, roaring sounds. Smaller cats, such as cheetahs and cougars, cannot roar. They make growling sounds, which are not as loud as roars are. Leopards are big cats, but they cannot roar.

Leopards growl. This black leopard is called a panther.

Lions and tigers are the only cats that can roar.

8

Gorillas let out loud growling sounds and beat their chests to warn other animals to stay away.

Hyenas make loud calls that sound like laughter. The sounds can be heard far away.

Wolves howl to stay in touch with their pack and warn other wolves to stay away!

Humpback whale songs

Not all sounds made by animals are warning sounds. Some sounds are made by male animals to attract female animals. The animals then **mate**, or join together to make babies. Humpback whales sing long songs that are made up of sounds such as high chirps, low moans, groans, roars, and snores! The songs last about fifteen minutes and are then repeated for hours at a time.

A male humpback whale may follow a mother and her calf to try to mate with the mother and to keep other males away from her.

male

calf

mother

Competing for females

Humpback whales not only sing, they also leap out of the ocean in great **displays**, or shows. They **breach**, or raise their bodies out of the water. Some whales smack their fins against the water's surface. The whales may do these things to compete for mates. Only whales know for sure!

This whale is slapping his tail against the water.

This male humpback may be showing its strength to females or the other males by breaching. Whales may also breach to warn boats that they are too close.

Bird songs and dances

Birds sing and dance to attract mates of the same **species**, or kind. Each bird species has its own song and dance. The dances are called **courtship dances**. Early in spring, a male bird sings or dances to attract a female. Together, the male and female will raise a family. The male also sings to tell other birds of his species to keep out of his **territory**. A territory is an area where an animal lives and finds food. The singer in the picture above is a bird called a lark.

This male crowned crane is doing a courtship dance for a female that it wants as a mate.

*Peacocks have colorful feathers. They spread out their feathers to show them off to the **peahens**, or females.*

This male blue-footed booby is doing a courtship dance.

13

Nests and other gifts

Male weaver birds build nests to attract females. The better the nest, the more likely a female will mate with a male. Weaver birds build nests that fool predators. They build several entrances to their nests and hide the real entrance so that predators will not be able to find it.

Male roadrunners bring gifts of food to female roadrunners. This roadrunner has hunted a lizard to give to a female that he hopes will be his mate. Why do you give gifts? Name three different messages you may be communicating with the gifts you give.

How to look bigger

Animals can make themselves look bigger to predators. They may also do it to attract mates. Some frogs, lizards, fish, and birds puff out their bodies. The frill-necked lizard usually holds its frill against its neck. It opens the frill to attract mates or frighten predators.

lizard's frill folded on neck

This lizard has opened its frill to scare an enemy.

peacock butterfly

Frogs puff out **throat sacs** to make loud calls to female frogs to let them know that they want to mate.

The false eyes on its wings make this butterfly look bigger to its enemies.

Frigate birds also puff out throat sacs to attract mates.

An anole's colorful throat sac is called a **dewlap**. Anoles use their dewlaps to attract mates or scare away predators.

17

I'm warning you!

Animals use the colors, shapes, and patterns on their bodies to warn predators. Patterns are colors and shapes that repeat. Animals with brightly patterned skin may send messages that their bodies contain **poisons**. Poisons can make the animals that eat them sick or even kill them. Brightly colored fish, snakes, insects, and frogs, such as these poison dart frogs, are deadly to eat!

poison dart frogs

*The butterfly on the left is a monarch butterfly. The one on the right is a viceroy butterfly. Both taste very bad to predators. These two butterflies are using **mimicry** to help remind predators that animals with bright patterns taste awful. Mimicry is looking like something else.*

viceroy butterfly

monarch butterfly

Viceroy butterflies have a black line across their back wings. Monarch butterflies do not have this line.

Ouch! That's sharp!

Some animals are covered with sharp **spines** that look like big needles. The **texture** of spines communicates that the bodies of these animals are dangerous to touch. Texture is how something looks and feels. How do you think these animals would feel if you touched them?

Lionfish have sharp spines that are poisonous. Their sting is very painful!

Hedgehogs have very sharp spines. A hedgehog can roll into a ball to protect its face when it feels afraid.

The spines of this porcupine are sharp and long. The spines will stick into a predator's skin and come away from the porcupine's body. The ends of the spines have **barbs**, or hooks, that are hard to remove.

19

Scent messages

Many animals leave behind special **scents**, or smells. Scents may be sprayed into the air, mixed with **urine** or **saliva**, or be rubbed onto objects. The scents are used to mark territory, identify animals that belong to a group, or lead other animals to food.

Cats, such as this lynx, mark their territories with urine and by rubbing parts of their bodies on tree trunks.

Ants use scents to recognize members of their groups and to let them know where nearby enemies are located. Ants also use scent trails to lead other ants in their group to food.

Red-bellied lemurs also use scents to mark their territories.

Skunks send very strong scent messages! When a skunk senses danger, it raises its tail, stomps its foot, and sprays. Now, that stinks!

Touch is communication

Many animals use touch to greet one another. Giraffes press their necks together, elephants use their trunks to say hello, and chimpanzees touch hands as a greeting. Many kinds of animals hug each other and greet one another with kisses. Some animals show their affection by **grooming** another animal, or cleaning its fur or skin.

Giraffes press their necks together to say hello or to show that they like each other.

This baby lynx rubs its mother's cheek to show love and to remember her scent.

Elephants greet one another by joining their trunks.

These three baby tigers are huddled together to feel safe. They were born just a few days before.

Even iguanas need hugs! These marine iguanas live in the Galapagos Islands.

Dolphins constantly touch with their fins. They touch to get to know members of their groups. Mothers touch their babies often to make them feel safe.

23

Mothers and babies

Some animals, such as frogs, fish, and many reptiles, do not look after their babies. Other animal parents stay close to their babies, keep them safe, and teach them how to find food. These parents and babies need to communicate with one another. They use smell, sight, hearing, touch, and body language to communicate.

Penguins make loud calls to locate their babies. The babies know the calls and can find their mothers, even among thousands of penguins.

eggs in nest

eggs hatching

Baby alligators and crocodiles make noises inside their eggs to let their mothers and other babies know that they are ready to **hatch**, or come out. The sound they make is "umph, umph, umph."

This mother monkey is grooming her baby. Grooming is cleaning the baby's fur of insects. It is also a way of showing love.

This baby giraffe is kissing its mother to show love.

Group communication

Animals that live in groups communicate to keep order in their groups. They communicate when they hunt or when they look for plants to eat and water to drink. They warn one another of danger. They also communicate when they play. They use sound, smell, and body language to communicate.

An angry wolf bares its teeth and growls.

*Wolves live in groups called **packs**. They communicate with one another by using body positions. **Dominant** wolves show that they are in charge by holding their heads up. The other wolves in the pack keep their heads and bodies closer to the ground.*

Dolphins often travel in huge groups called **schools** or **pods**. They communicate by moving their fins in certain ways, by swimming close together, by opening and closing their jaws, and by slapping their tails on water. Dolphins also make many sounds that have different meanings.

elephant trumpeting

Elephants live in groups called **herds**. The leaders of the herds are the oldest elephants. They know where to find food and water. Elephants make deep, rumbling sounds to let members of their herds know which way they are going and if other herds are heading that way. Some elephant sounds are snorts, screams, barks, roars, cries, and trumpeting.

27

Animals and people

Animals communicate with one another, and some also communicate with people. Pets usually live in people's homes and are a big part of their lives. Pets communicate with their owners to let them know what they want or need. Which of these pets wants a treat, which one wants to go for a walk, and which one wants to play? How does your pet communicate with you? How do you let your pet know what you want it to do?

Animal trainers

There are people who train animals to follow **commands**, or orders. Animal trainers use words and signals to teach animals how to behave or perform. They usually reward animals with food when the animals have carried out an action correctly.

Dolphins are very smart animals. Their trainers use sign language to teach them how to do tricks. They give them treats to reward them. Dolphins love to play!

Monkey messages

Monkeys are animals called **primates**. Primates are the most intelligent animals. Monkeys use sounds and actions to send messages to one another. They bark, howl, grunt, roar, and chatter. They also use body language. They jump up and down or bare their teeth to show anger. They hug and kiss to show love.

This young golden lion tamarin is calling to its mother.

Capuchins are the smartest monkeys. They have feelings that are similar to the feelings that people have.

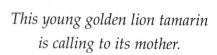

Diana monkeys make different sounds to warn their group of different predators. They can also understand the warning calls of other species of monkeys! Knowing these calls keeps them safe.

Macaque monkeys live in **troops**, or groups. Both mothers and fathers help look after their babies. These macaque monkeys are holding their baby close to protect it from predators.

Monkeys make loud calls to let others in their troops know that they have found food.

This monkey is not smiling. Monkeys bare their teeth to show anger.

31

Glossary

Note: Some boldfaced words are defined where they appear in the book.

body language Actions, motions, or behaviors that animals and people use to communicate

gesture A hand or head movement used for communication

mate (n) A partner needed to make babies; (v) to join together to make babies

mimicry A color, pattern, or shape that makes an animal look like something else in nature

pattern Colors and shapes that repeat

predator An animal that hunts and eats other animals

primate An intelligent mammal, such as a monkey, ape, lemur, or human

saliva Moisture in the mouth

species A group of closely related animals that can make babies together

territory The area that is claimed and defended by an animal, in which it lives and finds food

throat sac A pouch on an animal's throat that fills with air when the animal makes a sound

urine Yellowish liquid waste that is discharged from the body

Index

Printed in the U.S.A.—BG